I0472905

Eudaimonia

ISBN-13: 978-0692639061

Morgan Drolet
and
Shawn Sullivan

NEON BURRITO PUBLISHING

Morgan Christopher Drolet

Born in California. Comfortably desperate.

Shawn Michael Sullivan

Had a reading fort under the stairs in his room.

XLIX

eudaimonia was completed by the first day of
two thousand sixteen
which was, then, the furthest day in the
history of human existence so far (fuck
yeah)

world population was doubling in half-
century intervals (holy shit) ! !
at least seven billion people were living ! !
more than ever before (represent)

all numbers were up
including statistics related to
depression, hikikomori, alienation
plus, grave statistics which the news
mentioned to keep us informed

point is
people always flip out about their own time

always
and humans are still in their teens
they're not yet both highest volume and
furthest accomplished
as they're unable to fully solve an unhappy
problem with having to be human
that's all i'm saying, literally, peace

L

A woman in black uniform
Custodial housekeeping roomservice
Face made golden in the only spray of light
Under the bridge
Up on bunker hill
I watch her
Facing the rising sun
to the east
Her bare arms
    not young
uncovered in warming morning
Los Angeles
I watch her
hold some too small object
Black silhouette lips move
Pray to eastern gods
under the breaking dawn downtown
And she moves the too small object
to her lips
Offers it up and out
Bending at the knees in homage
At the entrance to a parking garage
Under a bridge
Up on bunker hill

LI

A young mother
Daughter's hair of woven pearls
Them running for the bus
Diapers in boxes
       chips dehydrated milk cereal
       non perishables
       files and folders
       plastic dolls
The black wire cart
stacked & secured by expert hands
a full foot higher than the mother's head
Beeping caution of the wheelchair ramp
Lowered
A balancing act up the gangway
Three stops
The scene reverses
A man with hair like Art Garfunkle follows
them with his eyes
Coiffure tingling
in the breeze from an open window

LII

recently i've been desiring to steer my plane
away from an absolute destination

since recently i've been flying my words into
absolute despair

and first of all what kind of destination is
despair what the fuck

second of all the flight is the best damn part
jesus christ

so many times i've landed in the wrong
places

it's absurd, in other words i've lived absurdly

which could condition me toward despair

but that's what i'm saying, too, i'm saying
i've still got plenty of gas

and i'm searching for new air traffic
controllers in new watch towers

and where i've been and where i thought i'd
go isn't on my mind

two thousand fifteen can rest in piss

LIII

He saw the glint
there
Under the red bench
Below the swift sky clouds
white and billowy morning quick
He stepped off the bus
Holding the turned down brim
the fedora against the wind
Approaching from the rear
Bending
Sliding the quarter across checkerboard square
concrete
Righting himself
Inspecting the printed metal as if
it was the first he'd ever seen
Into a pocket it goes
as the man himself plunges forward
Slowly

LIV

Sitting in my living room (tomb?)
Reading about Piere Renoir on my phone
        https://www.wikipedia.org
Having just read a portrait of him
  painted in the plain poetic words of Carl
Sandburg
So I'm learning about his rheumatism
His death
Always first scanning for the age of the
person
at death
Skipping to their final days
Obsessed with endings
I remember my coffee has been cooling
Room temperature being too low
this November
for hot drinks
I read an article
about the people who dismiss
Renoir
and probably others
For a lack of skill or
ability
They're maybe right

I remember a time
Seeing a long time ago
        maybe yesterday tomorrow or later
today
when I thought
        maybe needed to think
that things are better or worse for this/that
Wonder now
Is it just that things are good
for being
this or that
I hear a low incomprehensible voice
Immediately thinking some electronic device
some artificially intelligent operating system is
malfunctioning
Slowly realizing it's only two women passing
the window of my chilly couch
But first I thought it was a robot
The world is a different place now
Different days
than of Sandburg and Renoir
Still
Very much the same

LV

i read about dementia on wikipedia (omg)
i saw myself
FUCK
i became terrified
i considered my psychosis (with delusions of
persecution)
i felt light-headed and intensely worried
i laid on my futon

i remembered how it (wiki) said each
symptom of psychosis
and agitation/aggression
must be assessed and treated
independently of the underlying dementia

some long and awful minutes later
i remembered i'm not a doctor and neither is
the internet
and i always overscare myself by reading
medical stuff on the internet
and i thought about a person knowing one
part of himself is altered
a part of him is unknowable to himself

LVI

I am laying in bed now
Woken
Putting on a little Indian music
Barely heard
above the white noise wind
surging funneling whooping
Some bursts punching
Rattling the hunched old structure
around me
The quieting intervals
The gathering of breath
Vishwa Mohan Bhat wafting cresting
stuttering climactic through the room
Reeling in the current
The circuits of air intruding
through the frames of welcome open
windows
I am wrapped in bed and blankets
Too lazy warm to venture from this island

LVII

today was mellower because
when i left my apartment i wasn't even
searching for my worries

i ventured into my day without stressing
when people saw me
or pondering if and how other people
thought of me

since anyway that's me thinking of
myself
disguised as me thinking of others

and my mission today is to avoid
thinking about myself
since my memories bring my worries

discovering this day as it unfolds
while operating on a neutral, open level

allows the funny to be funny and the sad
to be sad
and all of it, this my life, is nothing to me
today but what it is

LVIII

i've decided to think about my life
and this is within my normal routine
of thinking about my problem after it's there
i should have thought about this way sooner

LIX

On a train headed south
through the rail yards
My back painted to the wind
A film crew slips by
Tingle Green paint on an old dodge
skin of an unripe Orange
The camera printed image of tires burning
Black lacerations on the concrete
The bone canal
dry, the LA River
Past a small pond of beached skiffs
Pastel paint chips slowly arching apart
Ditto the chapped leather seats
Cracked rivers and road maps
Creaking June Apollo
Boiling cup of bebop
Pleated ripple of oasis heat rays
mumble on the lipstick rails that
start and end nowhere
The abandoned tracks
like the dead collapsed veins

of the tapioca colored junkie
Who pours himself into a chair
in the shade at their feet
Each time
        and at each next station
the train stops
I look down at the tracks
Silent and still
We seem to be slowly sliding backward

LX

i concentrate on the breeze against my body,
which feels as if a mouth blows toward me
a hi top shoe rubs against my right ankle

later i do some reading, but mainly i think
about the writers' lives as filled by their
words
then i wonder if i should stream a movie on
netflix, but i don't

i lie on my futon for no reason but to pass the
time
so a short nap or two sneaks inside my day,
then i eat dinner alone at canter's

then when night comes my worries leave this
world with the sun
and while calmly listening to some of this
year's metal music releases

i read about the united states minor outlying
islands
i google image search the palmyra atoll

at midnight on my day off i feel tired and like
everything's already over

so i go to sleep, planning to wake at eight to
watch wetlands on netflix

except i wake from my sleep once from the
sound of nighttime rain
this confuses my body, which thought maybe
this had been another nap

for some long and lame minutes with closed
eyes i hear sprinkling
until my sleep returns, then early morning
beeps from construction vehicles wake me

so then i have to listen to fucking beeping for
some waking minutes
resulting in me trying to slumber until i rise
to get ready for work again

LXI

This middle aged cat in the fashion district
One leg dangles
        nub 'neath the knee
        like a sausage end
from a wheel chair strapped to a colostomy
bag
Yellow urine hanging in a bent tube
Second leg a scarred prosthesis
He shakes a blue box of baby wipes
rattle crack o' change
Below,
a little dogs head
Panting in the sun
I deposit 50 cents
Happy 4th
Thank you brother
2 doors down from his post
Filling a white styrofoam cup
        black coffee smoke pouring over the
lip
I wonder
Is he a vet
Well, a vet of something at least
Did he lose those legs
in his first foreign land ?

Fighting a war for freedom
he lost ?
When that bomb went off
like a million overzealous fireworks
Took his mobility
Left him to piss in a bag
On a corner
mission in action
prisoner of war for change
I went back
maneuvered another dollar in the kitty
"Good lookin' for ya boy."

LXII

i decided to listen to jay reatard while
walking out of my apartment

this decision arrived to me for no particular
reason
just a scroll down musicians in my ipod and
he happened
(a parallel to what will occur within my
thoughts)

in the beginning of blood visions i felt solid
and able to spot qualities that magnetize me
to this musician who died young
he died while he was living

then "nightmares" started playing and my
feelings spun as i heard him sing:
"seems that my dreams only come true
when my dreams aren't about you"

then i thought, he's my dude
we share a fight through this life

so he's dead but alive to me
similar to the relationship he makes me
recall

LXIII

"Talk to the Virgin Mary man
a One 8 hundred number 1-
800-85555555..."
That smell of distilled alcohol crept
through, around
the December air
I could guess that his black mustache was
soaked
or
maybe a vapor through the pores
Through the clothes wrapped in
layers so thick it was
hard to guess at his actual size
Maybe
he
Never had to trim the 'stache
Just let the high octane spirits nibble
away at its edges
Keeping it neatly clipped above the lip
Who is the talking for when no one's
listening?
Is it for the comfort of
knowing he's alive?
If he keeps on strangling the bottle, keeps
on rapping

with only that smooth beautiful glass as
audience
            when no one notices if he's here or
gone
            is frightened by his coming, relieved at
his going
Is this talking as proof, proof enough of
his existence?
Watching him wander off
Slumped
beneath the weight
of backpack bulging zipper seams
maybe we both wonder if he's really there

LXIV

nothing
then everything
then, nothing again
what
ever
that's fucking lame

keep living anyway
got my own reasons for why i'm living
i'd rather be talking about something else
yeah, awkward, my bad

in terms of godzilla
i most cherish the perception of him as a
nuclear catastrophe
a monster created by humans through the
dangers of science

(this poem is related to me feeling few people
give me reason to keep living these days)
(and i don't give myself a reason either)
(and these problems are related)
(i feel embarrassed, off topic and confused,
sometimes when i talk about this)
(still i keep living, you know, i'm not
ridiculous)
(perhaps the only way in which i'm not
ridiculous is i keep living)

LXV

it used to be that i felt life might get hard
then suddenly i'm here in the hardness and i
wonder where life is

my thoughts travel into realms unlike this
world
rather than traveling toward what this world
can be
i travel into the void

wondering when and how i can travel away
from it again
if i have before

LXVI

Sitting on a hard bench
outside of Cabanas Restaurente Salvadoreno
A small grey haired man takes a seat
Juan Ruiz
My hands are cold because it is cold out
Not just for California
but for any hands anywhere
At least sitting ones
I introduce myself at some point later
Juan Ruiz has lost he son
He has gone to see Star Wars
The ticket
For his dead son
was offered by the sons friend
Juan Ruiz took the bus downtown from
Glendale
He missed the 94
Was buying candy as he watched it pass
Through the window of a Walgreens
The bus didn't pass through the window
Juan Ruiz saw it pass on the street
So he took a different bus
Downtown
In an uncrowded "thee-ay-ter"

Watching Star Wars with his dead son's
friends
He has other sons
One in Georgia
Of his four sons
three went to war
The one who didn't is dead now
Another son lives in Las Vegas
Wanting still to "blow shit up"
To quote Juan Ruiz quoting his son
The one in Georgia is a farmer
Chickens, fruits, vegetables
22 acres on which he also raises bees
7 square homes have been built there
In Georgia
For the bees
His dead son was in college
His dead son rode a motorcycle
had a job
was paying for school himself
Juan Ruiz seems sad and proud
Talking about the young man
twenty-4
His love of nature
Climbing and cresting mountains
None of these things killed his dead son
who was riding his motorcycle when
death ripped through him
He doesn't cry
Juan Ruiz
    To strangers at least

Just rings his hands occasionally
They must be cold as well
He buried his son for $15,000
        "It's expensive to die"
in the plot at Forest Lawn Cemetery that was
meant for him
                "You shouldn't have to bury a child"
I cannot argue with that
I cannot imagine that
My mothers greatest fear
for many years
was seeing me put in the ground
We have lost track of time
Him and I
When his bus comes we shake hands
Cold hands a week before Christmas
I watch him
The bright white light of the bus
His patient face
headed back to Glendale
where he will walk 2 blocks home

LVII

then my thoughts shift into another
perspective
which rearranges for me the dynamics of my
entire reality

the perspective:
life is not only choosing to be happy
but choosing how to be happy

its deduction:
i often dwell on who i am not
instead of focusing on who i am

i wonder how long this perspective will burn
within me
and if when it goes out i can reignite it

so for a moment considering that i am
something
i think, well, that sounds okay
even when i'm not sure i'm considering
myself right
but, i mean, i could be thinking about
burritos instead

yep, then i think about a burrito because i'm
a little bit hungry

then later i mention this philosophy to other
people
and they stare back at me in silence

so this entire mechanism now worries me

LXVIII

"I used to work for a guy who chiseled wood"
He fumbles with the yellow
    a dirty glowing yellow
mesh backpack on the floor
Nestled between his sneakers

"A wood chiseler"
Trying to hold the large
    3' X 5' wood frame
    missing glass
    backer
and keep his goods
        Also, he chews a long pen shaped
        piece of metal, like a tire pressure
        gauge, missing the gauge parts
Which include a beach towel
A half empty bottle of Thrive cologne
From falling
as the bus comes to a burning halt

"A chiseler of wood"
He is compulsively now
Buffing frame with beach towel
His mouth does not stop
It is moving in union with his hands

Buffing
"Oh shit"
At Alvarado
"Coming through. Driver! Getting off."
Buffing
Maneuvering through sardines of people in
isle of bus
A trout fighting upstream
I watch him
Amongst those other denizens
Entrenched on the corner
Beverly/Alvarado
As he sets the frame atop a sneaker
Lighting a cigarette
Bouncing on ever elocuous lip

LXIX

person: "if you think it's easy being me, you
be me!"
other person: (laughter) "nahh, but for
real..."

a well-known description of me, within the
thirteen people who know me:
my heart is on my sleeve, and fact is i have
low numbers

so i don't want data sheets but heart sleeves
not numbers but remedies
whatever this means this appears to mean
me
which then also means
many people wouldn't dream of being me
either
and i'm like "..."

how many people do i not dream of
becoming?

and i'm like, wondering
hmmmm
is it only that when one thinks something
bad will happen that it does?
can that apply to the good as well?

does one always find the bad in the good and
the good in the bad
and can i focus on the good?

i'll let my yesteryear be a silent film
let it have been made by d w griffith
pretty solid, but we can do better

LXX

Passing a hobo camp
Small
Only 2 tents and a
pile of feeble goods collected
Of one tent I can say
I hardly noticed
Maybe it was green
Maybe that just seems like the
color a tent might be
The other blue
capped with a rain blocker
Violent red
On which read the plea
   "OUR FATHER, WHO ART IN
HEAVEN…"
Two or several
Maybe more slept
in those tents
this morning 7:53
Or maybe one was a chapel
A place for brothers of the road
Full of sacrament sacrifice songs
from the road
A call for protection
Written on tops of tents
in each camp corner and underpass
Where this city's 26,000 unwilling Franciscans
congregate

LXXI

it's not that i'm obsessed with the concept of
my death
as i'm at least not yet old enough, to be
obsessed with thoughts of my own death

what's taking (draining?) my efforts
what's exhausting my emotions (nailed it)
is me trying my damned hardest at being
obsessed with life

so when i talk of life i talk of death
because i try to talk about anything when i
talk of life
which can feel like anything, and sometimes
can feel like death to me
at least i think that, when i glance at
skeletons or during a bad day or whatever

in the receiving room while working i notice
these books made by other people:
a humorous graphic novel of irrational fears,
titled deep dark fears
vivas to those who have failed, poems by
martin espada
the haunted america faq ("do i believe in
ghosts? no, but i am afraid of them.")
a book on ufos, how to talk like an alien

amid this all sits behold a pale horse

and the cover to the poetry book sentenced
to life by clive james inspires my excitement
makes me realize i'm currently feeling less
alone

these material items with their helpful
covers
imbued with their personal meanings
in them my life feels to me quite realistic
and fantastically electric

here in los angeles i like and miss the
midwest, with its country emotions
which mean nothing in an ultimate sense
but mean something when you're there and
see them, feel them, live them
(same as most things and places and people)
god i fucking miss feeling like i live around
people
people partially made by trinkets and
antiques and country roads
people unafraid of what's outside their
homes they treasure

people with their bucket-hearts overflowing
with endless water (<-- edit?)

[or/and
i miss my youth, as writers tend to]

LXXII

walking to the gas station off Genesee
Smoking
Going to buy more smokes
Which i do
while smoking
It's been like this the last few days
Since the clear beginning of fall
when the weather turned
and it started to feel like drinking
But I'm not drinking anymore
So it feels like fall is now a time for smoking
I smoked weed before leaving the house
I'm tensed up from the cold in two jackets
alarmed by my unconscious tensing
I need to mellow out
This is one of my problems
The weed helps
Sometimes

LXXIII

when you mention the good i might think
you've forgotten to mention the bad
and
when you mention the bad i might think
you've forgotten to mention the good

it's like, what
is nihilism my goal, is that what's
happening?
do i hate you, myself, or both of us? what?
both, since we're in the same awful world?
(this part is me being snotty to myself)

sometimes conversations help, sometimes
they hurt
i'm working on not being a hypocrite, by the
way

i keep editing eudaimonia
while monitoring my personal eudaimonic
levels

i discover through writing my similarities to
people experiencing dementia
and learn i'd disqualify as an air traffic
controller for numerous reasons

am i as happy as my poems say i am?

well i don't think my poems portray me as
happy
and in this dark moment of admission i'll say
i'm not happy now, not very often
though i feel capable of it, and often find my
reasons for being down ridiculous
and repetitive
and may my moods and thoughts fluctuate
into non-repetitive realms of joy
even during repetitive days

morgan reminded me of our fire within us
when he proposed to me 'eudaimonic' as our
book's title
this word he'd learned as his dictionary
app's word of the day
we chatted about its definition
further inquiry was satisfied through
wikipedia

and, well, i don't know, i don't know
i can say for sure that i don't know
it makes me happy we've completed this
(once read this can only be true)
our third poetry book we wrote together
let this be our year of eudaimonia

still, to be honest, it's still december thirty-
first two thousand fifteen
this poem is set before the first poem, but it's
being written after

here in the final night of this year morgan is
at a show with an old friend
i texted a girl (whom i shouldn't have
texted?) and we chatted fine, and she has a
date
and there's no one one else for me to call
tonight for us to hang
i'll be going into my next year feeling alone
while being alone
what could bring me down is obvious, isn't
it?
i ask the person next to me, as in i'm asking
nobody

because i think i could feel down but want to
feel higher, i get high and look beyond the
obvious

when brett comes home i'm surprised to see
him and
me, myself, i start a conversation with him
about movies
i tell him carol was my favorite movie of the
year
tell him carol is in my heart as mad max is in
the hearts of others
(mad max is in his heart he tells me, yup)

brett tells me the longtime lounge singer of
canter's sings at midnight
she has the last few years he tells me

and i might go, i might not

i don't drink anymore, so bars can bore me,
and i have no real friend tonight
but i might watch a movie, which is where i
store some of my imaginary friends

i'm going to eat dinner at 88 chinese sushi,
it's eight now
i'm listening to black devil disco club's no
regrets, my song of this year
i'm bringing how to get into the twin palms
along with me
i'm thinking about watching juaja later
later i won't finish this poem because the
book is done by midnight
so what i'll do is a mystery to me now

LXXIV

Standing facing the chapel
Corner of Beverly and Liquor
The old man
switching the cane to his left hand as she
reached for his right
              Her blouse succulent red of sin
The other arm pours from his sleeve
caramel and yellow a fist clenched knuckle
white
The bells take up the weight of their silence
Beat it against the belfry walls
Returning it
spent and languid
The way a man finds the first grains of
shoreline and hope
After lost days of shipwreck

DON'T NOBODY KNOW NOTHING ABOUT THAT